Gabriel
FAURĒ
REQUIEM
1893 version

with the composer's original
chamber instrumentation

edited
with English translation
by
JOHN RUTTER
for soprano and baritone solo,
SATB chorus and instrumental ensemble (see p.4)

VOCAL SCORE

MUSIC DEPARTMENT

OXFORD
UNIVERSITY PRESS

PREFACE

'Hearing Fauré's *Requiem* as he intended it to be performed would be a revelation to most people.'

ROBERT ORLEDGE, *Gabriel Fauré*, p.110[1]

1. HISTORICAL BACKGROUND

Rather few of the countless performers and listeners who have taken Fauré's *Requiem* to their hearts can be aware of the long and complex history of its composition; probably still fewer know that the published version with full orchestra is far removed from Fauré's original, more intimate concept of the work, and was very possibly not even prepared by Fauré. The aim of this edition is to present the *Requiem* in a form as close as possible to Fauré's known intentions — though, unless new sources come to light, a completely definitive Fauré *Requiem* will remain as elusive as a completely definitive *Messiah*.

Gabriel Fauré (1845–1924) began work on his *Requiem* in 1887 purely, in his own words, 'for the pleasure of it'[2], though the death of his father in 1885 and of his mother two years later may well have given impetus to the composition. He was at the time choirmaster at the fashionable church of the Madeleine in Paris and gradually gaining a reputation as a composer, though much of his time was taken up with private teaching which he found uncongenial. He completed his 'first version' of the *Requiem* early in 1888, and the first performance took place under his direction on 16th January of that year; the occasion was the funeral service at the Madeleine of a certain M. Joseph Le Soufaché. This 'first version' (the only one for which any manuscripts survive) consisted of five movements, as follows:

1. Introït et Kyrie: choir SATB with divided violas, divided cellos, basses, timpani, and organ. Parts for 2 horns and 2 trumpets subsequently added, apparently in Fauré's hand. (Ms. 410, Bibliothèque Nationale, Paris)

2. Sanctus: (dated 8th January 1888) choir SATB with violin solo, divided violas, divided cellos, basses, harp, and organ. Parts for 2 bassoons, 4 horns, and 2 trumpets subsequently added. (Ms. 411)

3. Pie Jesu: soprano solo with (probably) divided violas, divided cellos, basses, harp, and organ. (Ms. lost; this movement known only from published version of 1900)[3]

4. Agnus Dei: (dated 6th January 1888) choir SATB with divided violas, divided cellos, basses, and organ. Parts for 2 bassoons and 4 horns subsequently added. (Ms. 412)

5. In Paradisum: choir SATB with viola solo, divided violas, divided cellos, bass, harp, and organ. Parts for 2 bassoons, 4 horns, and violins subsequently added. (Ms. 413)

This is not, of course, a complete liturgical Requiem (moreover the *In Paradisum* comes from the Burial Service); Fauré made a personal selection of texts, laying emphasis on the idea of rest and peace and omitting the Day of Judgement altogether. The instrumentation is restrained and sombre: Fauré may possibly have got the idea for his string group of divided violas and cellos with basses but no violins from the opening chorus of the Brahms *Requiem* (though Brahms was little known in France at this time). The organ exercises a continuo function: in the four movements surviving in manuscript it plays throughout, almost always containing the complete accompaniment, at least in its harmonic essence. The strings (probably no more than a handful at the first performance) therefore simply double the organ part for most

of the time, but this does not mean they are wasted: their richness and warmth adds greatly to the expressiveness of the music. Interestingly, it clearly did not worry Fauré that the timpani and solo violin each contributed to only one movement, sitting silent during the rest of the work; possibly, as at Bach's church, the parts were played by choir members who stepped into the orchestra when needed.

The *Requiem* in its original form continued to be performed at the Madeleine until the end of the century, but Fauré also prepared an expanded version for use on grander occasions. This expanded version, first given in January 1893, included two extra movements, the *Offertoire* (written in 1889) and the *Libera me*, both calling for baritone solo; the *Libera me* had been written as early as 1877 as an independent composition for baritone and organ. It is thought that it was for this 1893 performance that Fauré added the horn and trumpet parts to his earlier manuscript. The violin part for the *In Paradisum* may also have been added for this performance, though it seems slightly unlikely that Fauré would have expected a violin section (his manuscript clearly says 'violons') to sit through six movements waiting to play in the seventh. One possibility is that the *In Paradisum* was performed separately on another occasion at the Madeleine, perhaps at a service at which an orchestra including violins was available. The bassoon parts could well have been added under similar circumstances. The new *Offertoire* was presumably scored as in the published version, just for violas, cellos, basses, and organ; the *Libera me* was also presumably scored much as in the published version (with 4 horns, 3 trombones, timpani, and organ), though violins may not have been used: their part in the published version almost always doubles the violas. The horns, it must be noted, were essential in the *Dies irae* passage of the *Libera me*.

The third version of the *Requiem* — the familiar published one with full orchestra — received its première in July 1900 at the Trocadéro Palace during the Paris World Exhibition; the conductor was Taffanel. Hamelle published vocal and orchestral scores shortly afterwards; these are still in print exactly as issued then. How and why the third version came about is not entirely clear. Dr Orledge surmises that Fauré's publisher Hamelle urged him to prepare a 'version symphonique' in order to secure more performances — to turn the *Requiem* into a concert work, in fact. In a letter of 1898, Fauré promised Hamelle to prepare the score for publication, though no question of reorchestration was mentioned; Fauré asked, however, if he could delegate the piano reduction for the vocal score to someone else (his favourite pupil Roger-Ducasse was entrusted with the task). The evidence that Roger-Ducasse (or someone else) also relieved Fauré of the task of reorchestrating the work is conjectural but, I think, convincing: first, Fauré is known to have delegated the scoring of others of his works to assistants; second, he was burdened with teaching and administrative duties and may well not have had the time to rescore it himself; third, the published score has literally hundreds of misprints and other inaccuracies which the normally meticulous Fauré would never have let past had he been sent printer's proofs for correction. If he had prepared the score, he would have been sent proofs; the conclusion seems inescapable that someone relatively inexperienced both made the score and read the proofs.[4]

The scoring of the published version adheres in places closely to the original 1888 version, but elsewhere makes changes affecting dynamics, articulation, string bowings, and

1. London, Eulenburg Books, 1979
2. Letter to Maurice Emmanuel, March 1910
3. The *Pie Jesu* is known to have formed part of the original *Requiem* because it is listed on the title page.

4. In a letter of 1900 to Ysaÿe, who was shortly to conduct the Brussels première, Fauré laments the misprints in the vocal score.

indeed actual notes, frequently for the worse, I would say. Parts for flutes, clarinets and bassoons are added which invariably just double strands of the texture already there; the horn, trumpet, and bassoon parts are more or less arbitrarily recast from those of 1893, and the timpani are removed from the opening movement. Violins, mostly doubling violas, are added to the *Agnus Dei* and the *In Paradisum*, in the latter case not always the same as in the 1893 version. The manuscript of the 1900 version is lost, and there is no other documentary evidence of whether Fauré himself prepared it, and, if not, whether he approved it before it was issued, but I cannot believe that it is Fauré's work. Apart from the signs it bears of ineptitude and slipshod preparation, a full orchestral accompaniment (even one where the woodwind and brass have as little to do as here) strikes me as alien to Fauré's original concept of his 'petit Requiem', as he described it in a letter of 1888 to his friend Paul Poujaud. His choir of boys and men at the Madeleine was small, probably no more than twenty or at the most thirty voices, and would have been swamped by an orchestra of symphonic size. The accompaniment is essentially for organ, coloured and amplified by the other instruments; they must never be so numerous as to overbalance the organ and choir.

What, then, is the 'ideal version' of the *Requiem*? There can be no final answer unless new sources come to light, but my conclusions are these:

1. The two movements added for the 1893 performance (the *Offertoire* and *Libera me*) should be included.
2. The accompaniment should follow the 1888 version, but with two or (preferably) four horns as added for the 1893 version. The added trumpets and bassoons may also be used if players happen to be conveniently available, but they do no more than double other parts so can well be omitted. The timpani in the 1888 version can also be omitted. The solo violin (essential in the *Sanctus*) can take the added orchestral violin part in the *In Paradisum*. Violas, cellos and basses need not be numerous: as few as 5–4–2 would be appropriate with a small choir.

2. EDITORIAL CONSIDERATIONS

The four movements surviving in Fauré's 1888 manuscript (*Introït et Kyrie, Sanctus, Agnus Dei, In Paradisum*) pose relatively few problems. Fauré's manuscript is neat and accurate, the only ambiguities arising with the added horn parts and a few consequent adjustments where his final intention is not always absolutely clear. Where I have added or altered dynamic markings, these are shown in square brackets. Of the three movements extant only in the published version, the *Offertoire* is least problematic since its scoring (violas, cellos, basses, organ) is entirely consistent with the 1888 forces, and one can reasonably assume that it appears in the 1900 score exactly as Fauré wrote it in 1889; a few internal inconsistencies were easily corrected. The *Pie Jesu*, scored in the 1900 version for woodwind, harp, violas, cellos, basses and organ, is only slightly more problematic since the woodwind double the string parts and can be removed without loss. The *Libera me* (for 4 horns, 3 trombones, timpani, organ, and strings including violins) is scored for exactly the forces used in 1893, with the addition of violins which almost always double the violas and are dispensable. The parts for trombones (not used elsewhere in the *Requiem*) are dispensable too: they double horns 1–3 in all but eight bars in which they double the organ.
(*Note:* for a fuller discussion of editorial considerations, with select comparisons between the 1900 version and the earlier versions, see the November 1984 issue of *The American Organist*.)

3. THE ORGAN PART

Rather than make a piano reduction, I have in this vocal score shown Fauré's organ part exactly as he wrote it. Almost all of it is conveniently playable on piano for rehearsal purposes, and except in the *Sanctus* and the *Libera me* it contains all the essentials of the instrumental accompaniment. In these two movements where the organ does not contain the complete accompaniment, I have shown the additional music in the form of a second keyboard part which can be played by a second player on the same organ, or on piano. Perfectly satisfactory performances of the *Requiem* can be given in this form. Pedals should be used very sparingly in performances with strings; for performances with organ accompaniment alone, pedals can be more freely used, and I have marked [Ped.] in such places.

4. THE ENGLISH TRANSLATION

Whether to perform foreign-language works in the original or in translation is a matter of individual taste, liturgical custom, and, occasionally, strong prejudice. My personal feeling is that there is a good case for sometimes doing the opposite of whatever is your normal practice: if you are convinced that Latin is unsuitable for your choir, let them experience the beauty of this most musically settable of languages — the direct ancestor, after all, of Italian, the singer's language *par excellence*. If you believe that a composer's notes must forever be wedded to his original text, try a work such as the Fauré *Requiem* in English; you may be surprised at the immediacy of meaning it gains — in, for instance, such passages as the blood-curdling vision of Armageddon found in the *Libera me* or the sublime final prayer of the *In Paradisum*. My translation does not attempt to use the modern English of the ICET; the Latin texts of the Requiem Mass are poetic, and they probably had an archaic flavour even at the time they were written. Where I have been able to echo a phrase from Cranmer's prayer book or the Authorised Version of the Bible, I have not hesitated to do so. I have left the Greek phrases *Kyrie eleison* and *Christe eleison* untranslated since they were always foreign, even in the Latin liturgy.

5. TEMPO MARKINGS

The opening section (marked *Largo* in the original) is marked *Molto largo* in the published version; its recurrence is marked *Adagio* in the original, though the same tempo is presumably intended. Other tempo markings are the same in the original and the published versions. There are no metronome markings in the original. Those appearing in the published version are as follows: No.1 ♩=40, ♩=72; No.2 ♩=48, ♩=63, ♩=48; No.3 ♩=60; No.4 ♩=44; No.5 ♩=69, ♩=40, ♩=69, No.6 ♩=60, ♩.=72, ♩=60; No.7 ♩=58. If strictly observed they give a playing time of 31 minutes; allowing 3 minutes for pauses between movements, the performing time would be 34 minutes, which accords with Fauré's own estimate (given in a letter to Ysaÿe) of 'about 30 minutes or 35 at the most'. Size and acoustics of the building will affect tempo: it should be noted that Madeleine is a large, very reverberant church, and somewhat faster tempos might well be appropriate in a drier room.

I am indebted to Dr J. Barrie Jones of the Open University and to Dr Robert Orledge of the University of Liverpool for their invaluable advice in the preparation of this new edition. For the edition itself and for any errors in it I am, however, solely responsible. I gratefully acknowledge the financial assistance of the Open University in my research.

John Rutter
Cambridge, 1983

In addition to this vocal score, the full score is available on sale. The following orchestral parts are available on hire:

2 Bassoons	used in Nos. 3, 5 and 7, but entirely dispensable
4 Horns in F (3 and 4 dispensable)	1 and 2 essential in Nos. 3 and 6 (3 and 4 dispensable). 1 and 2 used in Nos. 1 and 7 (dispensable), and all 4 used in No. 5 (dispensable)
2 Trumpets in B flat	used in Nos. 1 and 3, but entirely dispensable
2 Timpani	used in Nos. 1 and 6, but dispensable
Harp	used in No. 3 (essential) and in Nos. 4 and 7 (dispensable)
Organ	essential throughout (plays from vocal score)
Violin solo	used in No. 3 (essential). May also play in No. 7 (dispensable)
Violas 1 and 2	essential throughout (minimum three 1sts, two 2nds)
Cellos 1 and 2	essential throughout (minimum two 1sts, two 2nds)
Basses	essential throughout (some *divisis*, but one player would be adequate)

This edition of the *Requiem* has been recorded by
the Cambridge Singers and members of the City of London Sinfonia
under the direction of John Rutter on Conifer CFRA 122
(cassette MCFRA 122, compact disc CDCFRA 122).

REQUIEM

English translation
by John Rutter

GABRIEL FAURÉ
Edited by John Rutter

1. INTROIT and KYRIE

© Hinshaw Music, Inc. 1984. Assigned to Oxford University Press 2016.
This edition published by Oxford University Press in 1985.

OXFORD UNIVERSITY PRESS, MUSIC DEPARTMENT, GREAT CLARENDON STREET, OXFORD OX2 6DP

6

2. OFFERTORY

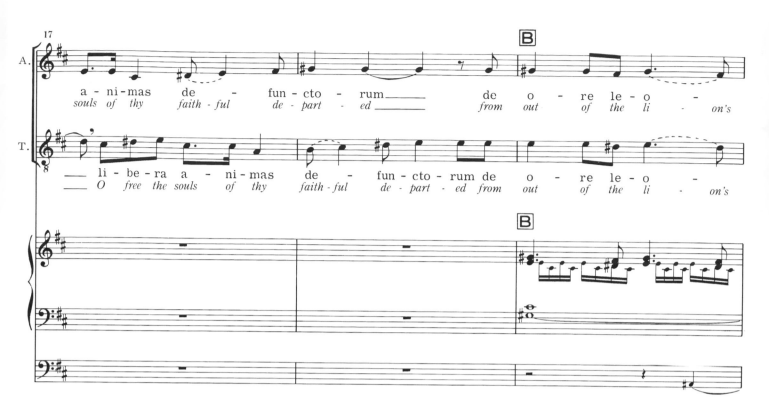

A. a - ni-mas de - fun-cto - rum_____ de o re le - o -
souls of thy faith-ful de-part-ed _____ from out of the li - on's

T. _____ li - be - ra a - ni-mas de - fun-cto - rum de o - re le - o -
_____ O free the souls of thy faith-ful de-part-ed from out of the li - on's

- nis,_____ ne ab - sor - be - at tar - ta - rus:_____ O Do - mi -
jaw,_____ lest they drown in the depths of hell: _____ Lord Je - sus

- nis,_____ ne ab - sor - be - at tar - ta - rus:_____
jaw,_____ lest they drown in the depths of hell: _____

[Ped.]

18

3. SANCTUS

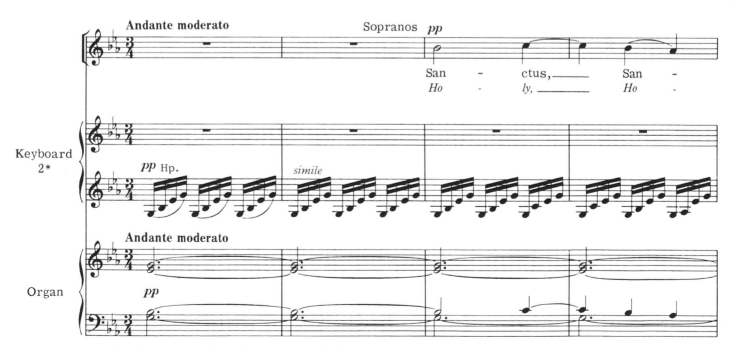

*Keyboard 2 part may be taken by a second player at the organ, or by piano or harp.

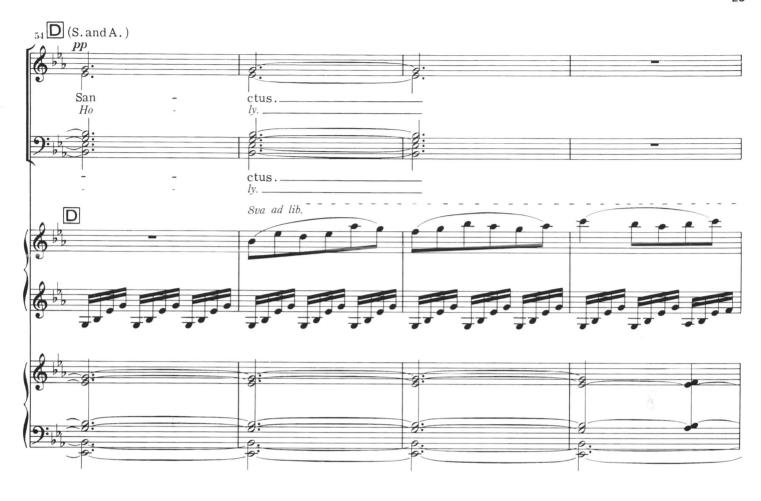

Sanctus.
Holy.

4. PIE JESU

5. AGNUS DEI

*Fauré notated the T. and B. parts of bars 50-52 and bars 58-59 in their enharmonic equivalents.

6. LIBERA ME

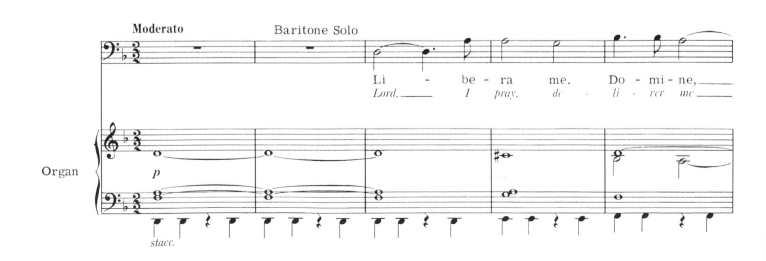

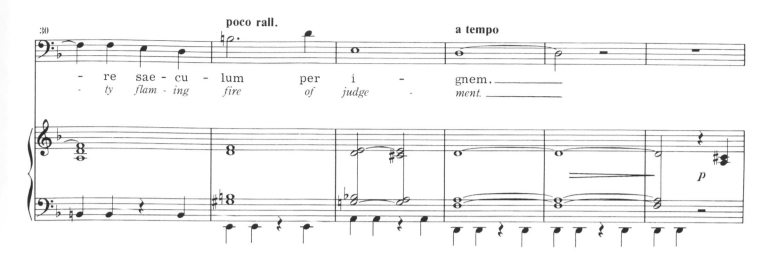

ma - gna et_____ a - ma - ra, a - ma - ra val - de.
ven - geance, *day_____* *of mourn - ing, of woe and bit - ter grief.*

Re - qui - em_____ ae - ter - nam do - na e - is
Rest_____ e - ter - nal grant them, Lord_____ our God, we

42

130

7. IN PARADISUM

*The r.h. staccato dots and l.h. slurs of the orchestral version are not in Fauré's manuscript.

48

Printed by Halstan & Co. Ltd., Amersham, Bucks., England